Other giftbooks in this series
Sorry
I love you madly
Little things mean a lot

Published simultaneously in 2005 by Helen Exley Giftbooks in Great Britain
and Helen Exley Giftbooks LLC in the USA.

Illustrations © Caroline Gardner Publishing, Liz Smith and Helen Exley 2005
Text copyright – see page 78
Selection and arrangement copyright © Helen Exley 2005
The moral right of the author has been asserted.

ISBN 978-1-90513-064-1 | 12 11 10 9 8 7 6 5

Edited by Helen Exley
Pictures by Liz Smith and Caroline Gardner

Printed in China

Helen Exley Giftbooks, 16 Chalk Hill, Watford, Herts WD19 4BG, UK
Helen Exley Giftbooks LLC, 185 Main Street, Spencer MA 01562, USA
www.helenexleygiftbooks.com

Go Girl!

A HELEN EXLEY GIFTBOOK

You can have anything you want
if you want it desperately enough.
You must want it
with an exuberance that erupts
through the skin and joins
the energy that created the world.

SHEILA GRAHAM

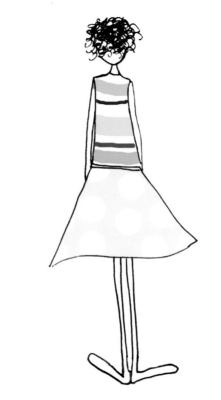

There isn't a train
I wouldn't take,
no matter where it's going.

EDNA ST. VINCENT MILLAY (1892-1950)

When a great
adventure is offered,
you don't refuse it.

AMELIA EARHART (1898-1937)

One can never
consent to creep
when one feels
an impulse to soar.

HELEN KELLER
(1880-1968)

I think that wherever
    your journey takes you,
there are new gods
    waiting there, with
    divine patience – and laughter.

SUSAN M. WATKINS, B.1945

Life is a great big canvas;
throw all the paint on it you can.

DANNY KAYE (1913-1987)

Wake up with a smile
and go after life....
Live it, enjoy it, taste it,
smell it, feel it.

JOE KNAPP

Twenty years from now
you will be more disappointed
by the things that you didn't do
than by the ones you did do.
So throw off the bowlines.
Sail away from the safe harbor....
Explore. Dream. Discover.

MARK TWAIN (1835-1910)

I might have been
born in a hovel,
but I determined to travel
with the wind and the stars.

JACQUELINE COCHRAN,
FROM "THE STARS AT NOON"

I love to wake up
and meet the day.
I think that life
is not to be wasted
or thrown away.

GOLDIE HAWN, B.1945

If you

can dream it, you can do it.

WALT DISNEY (1901-1966)

...warm, eager,
living life – to learn,
to desire to know,
to feel, to think, to act.
That is what I want.
And nothing else.

KATHERINE MANSFIELD
(1888-1923),
FROM HER "JOURNAL"

Creativity is inventing,
   experimenting, growing,
taking risks,
        breaking rules,
making mistakes,
      and having fun.

MARY LOU COOK

The word
"impossible"
is black.
"I can" is like
a flame of gold.

CATHERINE COOKSON
(1906-1998),
FROM "PLAINER STILL"

...there is no obstacle
you cannot surmount,
 no challenge you cannot meet,
no fear you cannot conquer,
 no matter how impossible
it may sometimes seem.

ERIN BROCKOVICH,
FROM "TAKE IT FROM ME"

You either shrink and hide
or you throw your shoulders back
and charge right in.
I learned that charging
felt more comfortable for me.

MINNIE DRIVER, B.1971

Never grow a wishbone, daughter

where your backbone should be.

CLEMENTINE PADDLEFORD (1900-1968)

You were once wild.
Don't let them tame you!

ISADORA DUNCAN
(1877-1927)

You've never
seen the Alhambra?
Or the walls of Toledo?
Or Venice? Ayers Rock?
Machu Picchu.
They are there,
waiting for you.
The places other
people have been.
Now it's your turn.

PAM BROWN, B.1928

Just knowing
has meant everything to me.
Knowing has pushed me
out into the world,
into college, into places,
into people.

ALICE WALKER, B.1944

Love bravely, live bravely,
be courageous.
There's really nothing to lose.
There's no wrong
you can't make right again.

JEWEL KILCHER, B.1974

...if a window opens
and the prospect pleases,
float through it;
that window
may never open again.

MIRABEL OSLER,
FROM "IN THE EYE OF THE GARDEN"

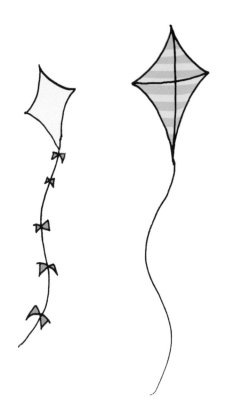

Some people say
I have attitude – maybe I do.
But I think you have to.
You have to believe in yourself
when no one else does –
that makes you
a winner right there.

VENUS WILLIAMS, B.1980

When anyone tells me
I can't do anything,
    why, I'm not listening anymore.

FLORENCE GRIFFITH JOYNER
(1959-1998)

The real definition of girl power
is having the strength
to be vulnerable and trusting.

JILL CUNIFF, OF LUSCIOUS JACKSON

There is
a microscopically thin line
between being brilliantly creative
and acting like the most
gigantic idiot on earth.
So what the hell, leap.

CYNTHIA HEIMEL, B.1947

There are hazards
in anything one does,
but there are greater hazards
in doing nothing.

SHIRLEY WILLIAMS,
FROM "THE FRIENDSHIP BOOK"

There is always a moment
when you have to act, despite your fears,
and jump out into the unknown.

HELENE LERNER-ROBBINS,
FROM "OUR POWER AS WOMEN"

Far away
there in the sunshine
are my highest aspirations,
I may not reach them,
but I can look up
and see their beauty,
believe in them....

LOUISA MAY ALCOTT (1832-1888)

What other reason
could there be for getting up
in the morning
except to set yourself free?

ANN MCMASTER

If you obey
all the rules
you miss all the fun.

KATHARINE HEPBURN (1907-2003)

My mother taught me
to walk proud and tall
"as if the world was mine".

SOPHIA LOREN, B.1934

*There's something
so vibrant and gutsy
about courage;
just do it.*

ANITA RODDICK, B.1943,
FROM "VOICES FROM THE HEART"

Don't be afraid to take big steps.
You can't cross a chasm
in two small jumps.

DAVID LLOYD GEORGE (1863-1945)

If you want to stand out, don't be different, be outstanding.

MEREDITH WEST

When I'm old

I'm never going to say,
"I didn't do this"
    or "I regret that."
I'm going to say,
"I don't regret a damn thing.
I came, I went, and I did it all."

KIM BASINGER, B.1953

If I had my life to live over...
I'd dare to make
more mistakes next time.
I'd relax. I would limber up.
I would be sillier than
I have been this trip.
I would take fewer things seriously.
I would take more chances.
I would take more trips.
I would climb more mountains
and swim more rivers.

NADINE STAIR

My favorite thing
is to go where I've never been.

DIANE ARBUS (1923-1971)

I haven't been everywhere yet,
but it's on my list.

SUSAN SONTAG

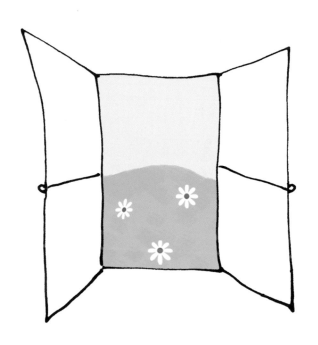

The future
belongs to those
who believe in
the beauty
of their dreams.

ELEANOR ROOSEVELT
(1884-1962)

Within each person
is the potential to build the empire
of her wishes,
and don't allow anyone to say
you can't have it all.
You can – you can have it all....

ESTÉE LAUDER (1908-2004),
FROM "ESTÉE: A SUCCESS STORY"

That perfect job –
fascinating work, charming people,
splendid salary,
opportunities ahead,
chances to travel.
It's out there somewhere.
Go look for it! It's waiting for you.

PAM BROWN, B.1928

Helen Exley runs her own publishing company which sells giftbooks in more than seventy countries. Helen's books cover the many events and emotions in life, and she was eager to produce a book to say a simple 'sorry'. Caroline Gardner's delightfully quirky 'elfin' cards provided the inspiration Helen needed to go ahead with this idea, and from there this series of stylish and witty books quickly grew: *Sorry*, *Go Girl!*, *I love you madly*, and *Little things mean a lot*.

Caroline Gardner Publishing has been producing beautifully designed stationery from offices overlooking the River Thames in England since 1993 and has been developing the destinctive 'elfin' stationery range over the last five years. There are also several new illustrations created especially for these books by freelance artist and designer Liz Smith.

Acknowledgements: The publishers are grateful for permission to reproduce copyright material. Whilst every reasonable effort has been made to trace copyright holders, the publishers would be pleased to hear from any not here acknowledged.